THE ART OF

HEALING

*12 Step by Step Meditative Art Exercises for Improved
Physical, Mental, and Spiritual Well-being*

BARBARA M. BUSTARD

The Art of Healing

12 Step by Step Meditative Art Exercises for Improved Physical, Mental, and Spiritual Well-being

ISBN: 978-0-578-83597-6

Barbara Bustard

©Copyright 2020 Barbara Bustard

TABLE OF CONTENTS

"ART IS A LINE AROUND YOUR THOUGHTS"

Gustav Klimt

Dedication

This book is dedicated to my loving wife, Judith. Thank you for always supporting me along my journey to become my highest, authentic self and to grow into the person I have the potential to be. You are my rock and my cheerleader. Your response to all of my ideas, no matter how far-fetched or crazy, is always a very sincere and loving "as long as it makes you happy." THANK YOU WITH ALL MY HEART!

Seasons of Life

Spring, Summer, Fall, Winter,
The seasons of our life.
Times of Joy
Times of Sorrow
Often times of Strife

Hold steadfast.
The winds will change.
Another season comes.
Begin anew.
Embrace the shift.
New life has just begun.

You have not failed.
You must evolve
   Into your truest self.
Life's journey often ebbs and flows;
Take time to rest upon the shelf.

When this time has passed,
  Arise refreshed and go along your way
To live your life with love and joy
For each and every day.

Barbara Bustard

"IF I COULD SAY IT IN WORDS THERE WOULD BE NO REASON TO PAINT."

EDWARD HOOPER

INTRODUCTION

Art is my refuge. For a lot of people, the idea of doing something artistic is frightening! There exists an errant mindset that to create art you must be talented, possess a natural gift or be specially trained. To create is an inborn facet of our being. We are more than our physical bodies. Art is the vehicle that can take your spirit on a healing journey. Creating allows us a safe space to express our anger or sorrow and release it to the universe to be healed. Through art we can also express our joy and thanks; we can make our dreams or ideas visible; we can express what we cannot speak.

This book is a guide for your Spirit's journey of healing, exploration, and expression. It may be balm for your Soul. Do not be afraid. Your Spirit is on this human journey to create, explore, experience, and learn through all that life brings us, good or bad, happy, or sad, pain and joy.

Just as each year bring seasons, so does life. We have seasons of Spring when we grow, learn, have new adventures, begin a new phase of life. There are Summer seasons filled with laughter, love, carefree times, and sunny days. Fall seasons are times of letting go, changes, transitions, and grieving loss. Winter brings us hibernation, rest, quiet, solitude, reflection, and healing to prepare for our next Spring. All these seasons carry with them emotions: joy, grief, uncertainty, peace, serenity. Our life seasons do not coincide with the calendar year and they do not always come in order.

We need to take time to listen to what our soul is saying to us. The combination of art and meditation allows our spirit to speak to us, to express our soul's journey, be it joy, grief, exhaustion, or a desire for a new path. This book is a companion for the journey, a way to allow your spirit to speak its truth.

For those dealing with situations requiring medical treatment, THIS BOOK IS NOT A SUBSTITUTE FOR MEDICAL CARE. It may, however, be a helpful accompaniment to medical care.

WE DON'T MAKE MISTAKES, JUST HAPPY LITTLE ACCIDENTS."

BOB ROSS

HOW ART HEALS

Studies have shown that just looking at art can release endorphins in our brains which produce a sense of well-being. Creating the art is even more powerful. When we create, we open new neural pathways in our brain. The more pathways, the better our brain functions.

Our brain is divided into the left and right hemispheres. The right side of the brain is the creative side and the left side is the analytical, logic side. Creating engages our imagination allowing us to feel hopeful and see all kinds of possibilities. When we create art, we are also constantly making decisions about tools to use, colors, how to make a sculpture support itself, etc. This engages our left analytical side. So, creating art improves our brain function, memory, and problem-solving skills.

But what about helping to heal the body? When we engage in creative activity, our mind relaxes and our stress level decreases. Stress is a major underlying cause of illness, so anything that can reduce stress is healing.

Engaging in creative activities has also been shown to reduce pain. When we are engaged in the creative process our focus is not on the physical pain in our body. We are distracted from the pain, and the pain becomes less noticeable. Hospital studies have shown that providing art opportunities to patients receiving pain medication, actually reduced the amount of medication they required.

As creative activity releases feel good hormones in our brain, it can help to lift the spirits of those suffering from grief, sadness, and depression.

Art helps people work through life events and illness. It provides a vehicle to express and release whatever emotions are present. It gives voice to things we cannot find the words for. Art provides an outlet to release our anger, fear, and grief.

Art gives us a window into our higher, authentic selves. As we engage in art and disengage with the physical world around us, our brain relaxes and creates the opportunity to engage with our higher selves. This is when our Spirit speaks to us, providing guidance, and insight into who it is that we have the potential to be. Art is a door to increasing our self-awareness.

Regularly connecting with our natural, creative selves helps us to live fuller, happier, healthier lives. The healing is in the process, not the results. Rekindle in yourself that joy you had as a five-year-old child when your artwork was hung on the refrigerator for all to see.

There are no mistakes in art. Just enjoy the process.

"ART IS AN EFFORT TO CREATE, BESIDE THE REAL WORLD, A MORE HUMANE WORLD."

ANDRE MAUROIS, FRENCH AUTHOR

How to Use This Book

This book is a resource for you to return to over and over for sparking your creativity, resting your mind, gaining insight, self-exploration and spiritual growth.

Each time you do the art exercises, you will have a different result, different insight, different experience, depending on your current life season, situation, or need.

After each exercise is a blank page for journaling or recording reflections of your experience.

The back of the book is an art journal. There are pages at the beginning labeled for the exercises that could be adapted to be done right in the book, if you choose. There is a traditional color wheel that you can color before making your own personal color wheel.

Following the pages for the exercises are blank pages for you to continue creating as you like! Writing is a great form of expression and insight. You could also create art journal pages combining drawing, color, and collage with your journal writing. Doodle, collage, paint, color, write, anything you like. Just create!

If you would like to try out the exercises first in the journal, most could be done with just pen, markers, colored pencil or collage. Be sure to separate the page you are working on from the remaining pages with a piece of cardboard or plastic to prevent bleeding onto the next page. You could also use watercolor and acrylic paints as long as you separate the pages. Just a suggestion, the Dollar Tree stores sell a 2 pack of translucent, firm but thin, plastic sheet cutting boards which you can easily cut to the size of your book and use for bleed proof separation. They are a staple of my art room. They can also be used as a reusable paint palette. If you let acrylic paint dry on the palette, it will peel off and can be thrown out rather than putting it down the sink.

If you choose to create in the book, when you have completed book size versions of the exercises, for your next experience, try using a larger canvas, either heavy watercolor paper, or stretched canvas and create some beautiful art to decorate your room or home.

The Clay meditation ball and the Splat painting are the only ones that cannot be adapted to be completed in the book. A visual prayer flag can be created in the book, similar to the painted prayer, but it would be best to create it in fabric and let it fly outside for the wind to carry its blessings.

AGAIN, these are suggestions on how to use the book. No rules. Just create! **THE HEALING IS IN THE PROCESS!**

"I MAKE ART WHEN I CAN'T GATHER THE WORDS TO SAY"

NIKKI ROWE, AUTHOR

SUPPLIES NEEDED

The following list of supplies is everything you need to complete all 12 art practices in this book.
They can be purchased at most art supplies stores and online. You may already have most of them.

Air dry clay
Acrylic paints
Watercolor paints (My favorites are liquid watercolor.)
Permanent color markers
Colored pencils
Ruler
Mixed media tablet 9x12 or larger
16"x20" canvas board, stretched canvas or heavy watercolor or mixed media paper
Pencil
Eraser
Sharpie Extra Fine Point or another brand
Old magazines, or printed out images and words these can be found easily through Google and printed out
Glue
Mod Podge
Balls in various sizes and textures
Aluminum baking pans or other container for holding paint

Audio versions of the meditations as well as templates for certain projects may be found at
https:/barbarabustard.com/resources

"Variety of form and brilliancy of color in the object presented to patients are an actual means of recovery"

Florence Nightingale

SILENCE YOUR MIND. PICK UP A PENCIL AND DRAW!

EXERCISE 1

PERSONAL EMOTIONS COLOR WHEEL

One of the first things you learn in art class is color theory. How to mix colors, the colors of the rainbow (light spectrum), primary and secondary colors and the meanings of colors. I love introducing young children to color theory. Their faces just light up when they see that the red and blue they put together turned into purple. The red and yellow magically became orange and the blue and yellow morphed into green. I use spin art machines for color mixing to add to the excitement! (I highly recommend them to all ages).

Color plays such an important role in our lives that many are not aware of. Color can affect our mood, energy, and heart rate. Some colors are soothing while others cause anxiety and agitation. Color therapy has been used to treat illness since the time of the Egyptians. Extensive studies have been conducted to determine the role color plays in our physical and mental health. There are specific colors which affect specific organs in our bodies. Through observation and study, certain emotions have been assigned to each color, however, an individual's personal response to a specific color may not necessarily fit the rule. We develop our color preferences and responses through our own personal experiences

While red may generally be associated with anger, as in the expression "I was so angry I saw red" and, if you had a negative experience involving someone wearing a red shirt, your response to red may be negative. Someone with a different significant experience with the color red may have an entirely different feeling about the color red. I for instance associate red with beauty, joy, and wonder.

Leaving church one day with two friends, we hugged goodbye as usual. I hugged the first friend and then hugged the second friend. While hugging her my field of vision behind my closed eyelids became filled with the most gorgeous, jewel tone red I had ever seen. It was so magnificent I did not want to end the hug too quickly because I wanted to bathe in that beautiful red. I said to my friend, *I'm seeing red!* When I left, she turned to the other friend and said *Doesn't red mean you're angry?* Clearly not in my case, she became my wife two years later! I still shut my eyes at times to conjure up that beautiful jewel tone red.

It is important to know what your feelings are for colors when expressing your soul's message in art. This exercise will guide you through a meditation and painting to understand what the colors say to you.

Meditation

Sit comfortably in a chair or lay down. Close your eyes and place one hand on your stomach. Breathe in deeply through your nose, all the way down to your stomach. Feel your stomach rise with each inhale. Slowly breathe out completely through your mouth until your feel your stomach fall. Again, slowly in through the nose, feel your stomach rise, exhale slowly through your mouth, feel your stomach fall. One last time, slowly in through the nose, feel your stomach rise, slowly exhale through your mouth until your stomach falls.

Visualize your sacred space. Where do you feel totally relaxed and safe? It can be anywhere you want. Is it in a lush green forest, or a warm sunny beach, or a special room? Wherever it is, settle into this beautiful, peaceful space. Lay down on the beach, sit under a tree in the forest, snuggle in your favorite chair, wherever you are, get comfortable and spend a few minutes experiencing the total serenity and safety surrounding you and holding you. In this moment, all is well in your world.

Now, focus on the movie screen that is on the back of your eyelids. It is filled with the color red. Look at the red filling the screen. Without filtering your thoughts, what is the first word or feeling that red evokes for you? How does red make you feel? Just allow whatever words, thoughts or feelings to flow freely and write them in your mental notebook.

Stay as long as you want with the color red. When you are ready, fill the screen with each color of the spectrum, noticing whatever thoughts or feelings each color evokes. Red, orange, yellow, green, blue, violet. Take as long as you like with each color, experiencing the feelings, memories, words, and thoughts that each color brings up for you and make a note in your mental notebook.

Whenever you are ready, get up and leave your special sacred space knowing you can return to this space at any time, and come back to the present and slowly open your eyes.

Materials

Watercolor or Mixed Media paper

Watercolor paints

Paint brush

Water dish

Sharpie Extra Fine Point - Black

Process:

On your paper paint an area in each color, any way that you like. You can just paint areas free form or create a sectioned color wheel, or start in the center and paint outward, again, no filter or judgment, just fill the paper with red, orange yellow, green, blue, and purple. After you have painted each color, recall your notes from your mental notebook and write them in or around each color.

Personal Emotions Color Wheel

Reflections

Reflections

EXERCISE 2

PAINTED PRAYERS

I keep a prayer journal. Most mornings, I rise early when light is just breaking, and I go to my prayer room/studio. I have a day bed in the room that has traveled with me for years. It is where I meditate, pray, rest, and read. In the early morning I enjoy the darkness and quiet before the cacophony of the day begins. No TV, radio, voices, traffic, or phones beeping. Only the sounds of the earth waking. Just the birds singing. I take out my prayer journal which is a 9x12' hardback sketch book. I form an intention for the morning's prayer or meditation. Sometimes it is a prayer for someone who I have heard is ill. It could be a prayer for some tragedy I learned about from the news. I might be struggling with discernment about a life decision, or job prospect. Whatever it is, I draw a circle in the center of the page and write the name or words in the circle. This becomes my painted prayer to the Divine. As I am creating this prayer, my attention is focused on lifting up whatever is written in the center. My Prayer Journal is bulging with painted prayers. It is beautiful to look at. Sometimes, when I am lifting up a specific person, I will do my meditation on a separate piece of paper so that I can give the original painted prayer to the person. I make a color copy to glue into my book. I leave the book open throughout the day to release the prayer into the Universe, and for me to see it throughout the day.

This form of meditation or prayer has helped me to get clarity about decisions I needed to make, helped me express grief, allowed me to express joy and thanksgiving as well. Sometimes things happening in the world are just so overwhelming and I feel helpless. Painting a mandala as a prayer lets my soul weep for things that I cannot control. A mandala creates a sacred space for expressing things that leave you with sighs too deep for words.

For this exercise the making of the mandala is the meditation.

Materials:

Watercolor or Mixed Media Paper
Watercolor Paints, colored pencils, colored markers (your choice)
Pencil
Ruler
Sharpie Extra Fine Point
A small item to make a circle, something about the size of a quarter

Process

Using your ruler, draw a line very lightly with your pencil diagonally from one corner to the opposite corner. Repeat from the other two corners, creating an X. Next, line the ruler up with the center of the paper, the spot where the lines forming the x cross, and make a vertical line from top to bottom and a horizontal line from side to side through the center of the x.

Using whatever you have to make a circle, place the item in the center of the x, and using the Sharpie, trace the circle. From now on, you will be using the Sharpie, not your pencil.

You may already know what you would like to write in the center of your mandala. If so, write it now. If not, sit quietly and take three deep cleansing breathes. Slowly breathe in through your nose and exhale slowly through your mouth. Close your eyes and let your thoughts go. What intention, prayer or question do you want to release to the Universe? When you know what you want to pray or meditate on, write the word, or name in the circle.

Working out from the center, connect the lines with any design you want, just make sure that you put the same design in each section around the circle. Continue working out from your fist design with other connecting lines, around the circle, making sure that you repeat the design in each section of that row. Continue out as far as you want.

When you are finished, erase the pencil lines and paint or color your mandala however your like. You can paint each individual section in a pattern or if using watercolors, let them just fill the entire mandala with color. Add words if you like.

Painted Prayer/Meditation

2015

Reflections

Reflections

EXERCISE 3

THE WINDING PATH

Sometimes our journey through life seems to be filled with wrong turns and dead ends. There have been times that I was sure of the path I was taking just to be devastated further down the road. However, looking back on these times, I see that if I had not taken that particular path, even though it did not go where I expected, I would not have arrived where I am, or had experiences along the way that were wonderful, educational, sometimes very painful, but all gave me some knowledge to carry with me. When reflecting on the various paths my life has taken so far, I often think about the words to Rascal Flatts' song "Bless the Broken Road" (originally by The Nitty Gritty Dirt Band):

I set out on a narrow way many years ago.

How true is that? We map out our path for where we are going and we have blinders on, staying on the narrow path. Then something happens!

But I got lost a time or two.

Wiped my brow and kept pushing through

We all get lost, don't we? Wiping our brow and pushing through takes courage.

This song is about finding love, but it applies to finding our way in life as well.

This much I know is true

That God blessed the broken road

That led me straight to you

Depending on your spiritual practice, change the word God to Spirit, Universe, the Divine, or whatever you use for naming your Higher Power. Then, change the word "you" to "where I am"

The Universe guides us through life, not always in a straight and narrow path, but without the twists and turns and detours, we may miss something that we needed to experience on this earthly journey. It is helpful to reflect on what we thought were wrong turns, dead ends, and detours we have taken and see how it all goes together to bring us to where we are and where we are still going.

I know that if I had not had what I thought to be wrong turns, dead ends, and detours, I would not be where I am now, which is not at all where I expected to be, but is where I am living fully into who I am. I often say, I feel more like myself than I ever have!

Materials

Watercolor or Mixed Media Paper
Black Permanent Marker
Sharpie Extra Fine Tip or Ball point pen
Watercolor paint, colored pencils, or markers

Meditation:

Sit comfortably, close your eyes and take three, deep cleansing breathes. Breathe in through your nose and out through your mouth, slowly and deeply. Do a body check from your feet to your head and let go of any tension.

You are standing at the entrance to a walking trail through a beautiful forest. Begin walking along the trail, noticing all the beauty around you. Just follow the trail where it leads as it curves through the trees. You come to a fork in the trail. Choose a path and begin to follow it. You notice a piece of paper on the side of the path with your name on it. Pick it up and read the message to you from Spirit. Hold it to your heart and absorb the message of love and guidance that Spirit is sending you.

You realize that this path is one you have taken before in life which you thought was a wrong turn. Follow it and reflect on where it led you, remembering the note you have from Spirit that you are being loved, supported and guided on your journey. At the end of this path is another note. Pick it up and read it. What is Spirit telling you about this road you took and where it led you? Ahead of you are other paths, all are paths you have taken before and each one has a note for you from Spirit. Go down each path and read the message Spirit has given you about your journey so far. What new experience have you had as a result of having taken this path? What knowledge did you receive from this broken road?

When you have arrived at the end of your broken roads, there is one more message from Spirit. Pick it up and read it. What is Spirit telling you about your path forward? As you turn and walk back along the path to exit the forest, reflect on what Spirit has told you and feel surrounded by love, support, and guidance. When you are ready, slowly open your eyes and return to the present.

Process

Using the permanent marker, begin on one edge of your paper and draw a line to another edge of the paper. Continue making lines from each edge of the paper to another edge of the paper. Make your lines curvy, straight, looping, and angled.

Use the Sharpie to label the paths with life events. Write any messages or insights you received during your walk in the forest along the lines or inside the areas created by the crossing lines of your paths.

Using your choice of watercolors, colored pencils or markers, color the sections created by the intersection of the lines.

When you are finished, look at the beautiful, colorful life you have had!

The Universe blessed the broken path that led you to where you are.

The Winding Path

Reflections

Reflections

EXERCISE 4

THE CLAY MEDITATION BALL

When I was 2 1/2 years old, I was adopted. The story I was told by my adoptive mother went as so. My biological mother was this first cousin once removed to my adoptive mother. In other words, my biological mother was the daughter of my adoptive mother's first cousin. My biological parents were getting divorced and my adoptive mother offered to "help with the girls (my sister and me) in any way". One day my biological mother called and said: "you can have them." According to my adoptive mother, when she went to pick us up my biological mother just handed us over and waved goodbye! I have always struggled with the knowledge that I was so disposable that my own mother would just give me away so easily. This was especially so after I became a mother myself. When my two sons were close in age to the ages of my sister and I when we were given away, I would look at them and could not imagine just handing them over to someone else.

My childhood looked ideal to the outside world but, my adoptive mother was not at all nurturing or maternal. Quite the opposite in fact. She was physically, verbally, and emotionally abusive. I often wondered why God would allow children to be given to someone who clearly did not want children. My consolation would be to tell myself that my current situation must be better than it would have been.

From childhood, I had an artist's spirit. I wrote poems. I carved a horse head in a discarded block of wood using a screwdriver and hammer. I always drew the picture in the back of magazines to see if I would be accepted for mail order drawing lessons. I painted one day in elementary school that lit a spark in me. I think it was a summer program and the teacher showed me a potter's wheel. It was in a little alcove in the teacher's office. The moment I saw that potter's wheel and learned what could be created with it, began my yearning to work in clay. That memory stayed with me for many years. It was not until I was in my 30s that my yearning desire to learn   the art of working in clay was realized.

My youngest son was attending preschool at the Community College and I decided to complete my AA degree which I had aborted years ago. The only credits needed to complete the degree were electives. Looking through the course offerings, I noticed ceramics classes listed. I was surprised to see that you could earn credits for painting those little ceramic figurines that were so popular when I was a kid. Reading the course description though, I discovered that ceramics was the art of clay: hand building, throwing on the potter's wheel and sculpture. I took every class I could. I was in love with working in clay.

Clay became my therapy. It was how I could feed my soul, relax, release anger, and express my true self. For 20 plus years I was a potter and ceramic artist. Often, I felt a deep spiritual connection with the clay. It was as if Spirit was creating through me, using my hands to form the clay. Isaiah 64: 8 resonated through my being. "Yet oh Lord you are our Creator, we are the clay and you are our Potter. We are the work of your hand." So, it was no surprise when clay was the means for me to bring into form a major revelation.

One day when I was about 40, doing breathwork in yoga class, the teacher related that when done correctly, this breath would sound like being in your mother's womb. When she made this comment my immediate thought was "How would I know what that sounds like? I was never there!" Now of course I realized intellectually that I existed prior to my adoption, but that part of my life was a total blank. The fact that I had never seen a picture of myself prior to age of 2 1/2 combined with the childhood memory of my "mother" yelling at me "Thank God you're none of my blood and never will be", had created a total disconnect to anyone having given birth to me. Several years later my life was on a different path. I was in the process of discernment for ordination and was in Spiritual Direction. When I conveyed this story to my spiritual director, she was not pleased at all with my lack of connection and informed me that I did not accept that I was a child of God.

Driving home from our meeting I was furious! How dare she say that to me! Then out of nowhere I am reciting Psalm 139:12,14,15. The strange part was that I was not a bible scholar! I did not really know the Psalms numbers or verse and was not able to recite them from memory. Nevertheless, I heard "for you yourself created my inmost parts/ you knit me together in my mother's womb/ my body was not hidden from you while I was being made in secret and woven in the depths of the earth/your eyes beheld my limbs yet unfinished in the womb" coming through clear as day! I was ecstatic! I got it! It did not matter the people involved or the secrets kept. God had been working this clay from the start. It was God that created me and was with me even if I had no memory or proof of my being. This clay was formed in God's womb and that is where the journey began. Having come to this revelation, I knew I had to create something to commemorate it.

As soon as I got home, I went to the studio and created a hollow ball of clay on which I engraved the words of Psalm 139. That ball is constant reminder that I am somebody's child. I have made many meditation balls since that first one, some for inspiration, some for grief, inscribed with the names of loved ones, and others for joy and celebration. Each one has been a powerful healing tool, through the meditative creation process as well as holding it, reading it, and feeling its weight in my hands for prayer or meditation. Now it is time to guide you in creating your own meditation ball.

Materials

1-2 lbs. of air-dry clay (available at craft stores or online)
A small dish of water
A small dish of vinegar
A toothbrush
A toothpick
Alphabet rubber stamps or pencil with a rounded point
A small dish of corn starch
Parchment or waxed paper for your work surface

You will begin with a meditation and move directly to creating the first pinch pot as a part of the meditation. **Before beginning the meditation, read through the entire exercise first to understand how to make a pinch pot. Then begin.**

Before starting the meditation, form two balls of clay using ½ to 1 lb. of clay for each ball. Form a rough ball in your hands then roll it around on the table with the palm of your hand until you have a fairly round ball.
(Note, remove your rings before you begin!)

Meditation

Sit comfortably in a chair with your feet flat on the floor. Holding a ball of clay in your hands, place your hands in your lap. Keep your hands still in your lap and just let the clay sit in your hands.

Close your eyes and take three deep, cleansing breaths. Focus your mind's eye on the soles of your feet. Feel the floor supporting your feet. Release any tension you feel. Slowly, taking time to check in with every part of your body, acknowledging any sensations you are feeling and releasing any tension being held, move from your feet, to your ankles, lower legs, thighs, buttocks, stomach, lower back, chest, neck, back of your head, top of your head, your forehead, eyes, nose, mouth, down to your shoulders, your upper arms, your fore arms, and without moving them, focus on your hands, your fingers, and then notice the sensation of the clay in your hands. Notice its weight, its temperature, its texture. With your inner eye, stay focused on the clay and make an intention, prayer, desire that you want the clay to hold.

Now, with your eyes remaining closed, hold your clay in your non-dominant hand and using your thumb from your dominant hand, push it into the center of the ball stopping about ½ inch from the bottom. Be careful not to push all the way through your clay. Squeezing gently with your thumb inside and your fingers on the outside, rotate and squeeze continuously around the opening until you have a bowl form. Be careful to leave the wall of your bowl at least ½ in thick. When you are satisfied with your pinch pot, and you are ready, slowly open your eyes.

Process

Make your second pinch pot, keeping the size and thickness as close as possible to your first one. Check that the edges of your pots match up when placed on top of each other.

Dip your toothbrush in the vinegar and scrub the lip of each pot. Place the pinch pots on top of each other and using your finger, move clay from one pot to the other to seal the connection. This is not smooth and pretty. Make sure to join clay from each pot to the other.

Cupping the ball in your hands, pat it and roll it until it is round. Place it on the table and roll it with the palm of your hand until you have a fairly smooth round shape. If it has small cracks and rough areas, dip your fingertip in water to smooth them. If it continues to crack slightly, poke a small hole with a toothpick to release some of the air inside.

Set your ball aside on the parchment or wax paper until it is firm but not dry. If you are leaving it overnight, cover it with a piece of plastic so that it does not get too dry.
Using either alphabet stamps or a pencil, or both, inscribe your ball with whatever is meaningful for you. Carve designs with the pencil if you wish. When using stamps, dip the stamp in corn starch then tap off the excess before pressing in the clay. This will keep it from sticking. Smooth any sharp edges from carving by dipping your fingertip in the water and gently rubbing the edges.

When your completed ball is dry, which could take as long as a week depending on the humidity, add color if you wish, using acrylic paint.

Reflections

"We are all jars of clay, fragile and poor, yet we carry an immense treasure."

Pope Francis

Meditation Ball

Reflections

Reflections

EXERCISE 5

RUACH – BREATH OF GOD

In our lives we go through many seasons. Not the calendar seasons, our life seasons. In spring seasons, we embark on new things, new life, birth ideas and intentions. In summer seasons we nurture and grow and bloom. Fall seasons are a time to let go of the past. We mourn and we move into Winter where we have time to heal, rest and hibernate so that when our Spring comes, we emerge rested, refreshed, and vibrant. The breath of God, Ruach, hovers over us in all seasons. This is a Spring season meditation for a time when you are ready to embark on new adventures or phases of your life. Remember, life seasons do not follow the calendar seasons.

Materials:

Mixed media or watercolor paper

Black India ink or watered-down acrylic paint

A straw

Watercolors

Sharpie Extra Fine Point or ball point pen

Meditation

Sit comfortably, feet flat on the floor, hands resting gently in your lap. Take three deep cleansing breaths and let all stress release from your body.

It is a warm Spring day and you are relaxing in your favorite spot. You feel the sun on your skin, wrapping you in warmth and comfort. You are totally at peace.

A warm breeze begins to blow over you. The breeze comes from behind you and brushes past you, just kissing the side of your face. It blows past you then turns and comes back again gently blowing by you. The breeze is slowly and gently swirling around you. It is warm and comforting. It brushes by your ear again and whispers to you. This is the breath of God speaking to you. You are totally enveloped in love and warmth. Listen to the breeze as it envelopes you in love and whispers to you. What messages are you hearing? Take them all in and hold them in your heart, knowing that Spirit is guiding you to your best life. Stay with Spirit as long as you want. When you are ready to return to the here and now, hold the messages you received from Ruach in your heart. Deeply breathe in all the love and peace you are surrounded by and as you breathe out, thank Spirit for this time. Slowly open your eyes and remaining peaceful and meditative, begin your painting.

Process

Using your straw dip into the black ink and cover the tip of the straw with your finger to capture some ink in the straw. Keeping your finger on the tip of the straw, hold the straw over the paper and release your finger to drop the ink on your paper. Blow the ink with the straw all around your paper, turning the paper so that the ink blows in different directions. Keep adding ink and blowing it around the paper until you feel finished. Using watercolors, paint the sections created by the windblown ink. Use the Sharpie or pen to write any messages received from Spirit along your path, or in the sections.

"Calmness is the living breath of God's immortality in you."

Paramahansa Yogananda

Ruach

Reflections

Reflections

EXERCISE 6

FINGER LABYRINTH WALK

I am writing this book during the COVID-19 pandemic. For most people our normal daily routine has changed drastically. We are under a stay at home order to decrease the spread of this highly contagious coronavirus. Everyone who can, is now working from home. Those whose jobs were not conducive to working from home are now unemployed unless they are considered essential employees working in health care, grocery stores, and construction. Schools are closed and children are being taught online. There is now a new normal and when this pandemic ends, and we can resume "normal" life, it will be another new normal. Life will not be the same as it was.

For me this has been a season of Winter in my life. A time to rest, reflect, hibernate, and prepare for the new Spring of post pandemic life. During this time, I have become a published author, having written a chapter for The Ultimate Guide to Self -Healing Techniques. That experience rekindled for me my desire to write this book which I began at least 15 years ago.

During this time, my work schedule has dramatically changed. I already worked from home as an independent contractor teaching art in private homes, preschools, senior living apartments, extended day visual art magnet programs in public high school, monthly paint nights at a local restaurant, birthday parties, painting parties and private lessons in my home as well as participating in art fairs and festivals with my fused and cast glass art. All of those sources of income abruptly stopped with the exception of some online private lessons for several of my students. Most of these jobs will restart when it is safe to gather again.

During this quieter, calmer time, I have started focusing more on Art for Body, Mind, and Soul, my meditative healing art sessions. I have written this book and have plans to write a series. I am enjoying the slower pace of not running all over from one job to another as I did before the pandemic. I am thinking and visualizing ways to take my passion for combining art with meditation and spirituality on the road with workshops and retreats while still planning to resume all the other avenues of art I already teach and share. I share all of this as it is pertinent to the lesson I learned from this exercise.

Throughout quarantine, I have been having Zoom lessons with some of my students. One has been doing meditative art sessions. The week that we did the labyrinth exercise, which is this chapter that you are now reading, I had an unexpected experience and received a very clear message!

The labyrinth is a spiritual centering tool. They are usually walked but can also be done by letting your fingers do the walking. The labyrinth is not a maze. It is a guided path of winding back and forth turns that lead to the center where you take time to be still and listen to you Soul. You then wind your way along the path back out, reflecting on any messages received. You just stay on the path and you do not get lost. I have walked the labyrinth many times both with my feet and with my fingers on any of my collection of finger labyrinths. I just focus, follow the path with my fingers or stylus and wind my way to the center, clearing and relaxing my mind. I pause as long as needed in the center to receive whatever messages the Universe has for me and then I follow the path out, winding my way back to the entrance as I reflect on what I have received.

This particular day I found myself feeling very unsettled. I had explained to my student to make an intention or prayer at the entrance, follow the path to the center, pause and receive, then reflect while following the path back out to the exit. However, on this particular day, I was unable to clearly form an intention at the entrance, so I decided to just move on with the journey and get some clarity along the path. However, that did not go as planned. I could not manage to follow the path. I kept getting lost. I would trace the path with my finger and somehow kept going backwards and forwards but not actually moving along the path toward the center. I started over several times. Getting lost on the labyrinth had never happened to me before.

As I stated above, a labyrinth is not a maze. It is a guided path! I considered the possibility that this image which I downloaded from the internet and printed out, might be incorrectly drawn. Maybe that was why I was having such difficulty. Finally, I decided to start in the center and paint my way out, as we were going to paint the labyrinth after our meditation anyway.

By using the paint, I could see where I had traveled and see if this labyrinth image was, in fact, correct. I painted my way out without any trouble. The labyrinth was not the issue.

I took my brush and spread out the trail of paint I had squeezed along my path. It was more paint than necessary and in spreading it out along the path, the paint also covered the lines marking the path. They were black and still visible under the translucent paint, but the degree of visibility varied with the thickness of the paint in any specific area. Looking at the painted labyrinth I thought *I have to define my path.* I grabbed the black paint to go over the black lines of the labyrinth to make them more visible. It only took a couple strokes of black paint on those lines for the message to be clear. I HAVE TO DEFINE MY PATH! That was the message of my confusing labyrinth walk this morning.

Message received. I need to define my path for when this pandemic is over and a Spring season of my life follows this Winter season of quarantine. I need to define what it is that I really want to continue doing. What has to be left dormant in Winter to make way for new life in the post quarantine Spring? I need to decide what to let go of, what has run its course and can be released so that I can add the new things I want to pursue, the things I am passionate about. Even though I thought my experience on the labyrinth was not successful, my Spirit was giving me the path to receive the message I needed. I hope your labyrinth walk reveals to you what you need.

Materials

printed labyrinth on cardstock or heavy paper. Pdf can be found on my resources page

https://barbarabustarad.com/resources

your choice of any combination of watercolors, colored pencils, markers

a quiet place

Meditation

Begin by forming an intention, prayer, or request. Acknowledge with a Bell or nod when you are ready to enter. Follow the path with your finger. When you arrive at the center pause and receive any messages or insight the Universe has for you. Stay as long as you like in the center of the labyrinth. When you are ready, exit and follow the path, retracing your steps back to the entrance. Acknowledge your experience with a bow or a thank you

Process

Now remaining meditative, gather your paint or whatever medium you choose, and follow the path again with the painted colors. You may want to write words or messages and add images to your labyrinth. However you choose to embellish the labyrinth to reflect and remember the message you received is fine.

Finger Labyrinth

Reflections

Reflections

EXERCISE 7

WEEDING THE GARDEN

(Note to the Reader: Chapters 7, 8 and 9 can be done as a series or individually as needed)

Each year when the temperatures turn warmer, gardeners get excited to plant their new crop of vegetables and flowers, but first they must pull out weeds and dead plants from the last year to prepare the soil for new growth.

There are times in our lives when we must also pull the weeds and clear away what are no longer life-giving parts of our lives. We must pull out weeds and clear the dead plants to be able to have room to blossom fully.

Materials

watercolors, markers, colored pencils, any medium you desire
mixed media or watercolor paper
Sharpie Extra Fine Point

Meditation

Get comfortable. Take 3 deep cleansing breaths. Let all thoughts go. Relax your body. Check in to see if you are holding tension anywhere. Relax your shoulders if they are up around your ears, relax your jaw, release any tension you are holding in your body. Focus on your breathing and release any thoughts.

You are standing in the garden with your gardening gloves and boots on and notepad in hand for sketching out your plan. You have a plan and vision for the beautiful garden you will plant. You look around and see that the garden is overgrown with weeds and covered with dead plants from previous years. You will have to clear away the dead and pull the weeds to make room for your new garden.

Walk through your garden and notice all the weeds and the dead plants left from last year. What are they? What are the weeds in your life that will choke out your vision? What is no longer viable to leave in your garden and must be cleared or set aside for now in order for your new garden to grow? Walk through the garden of your life and study the weeds. What are they? What weeds in your life need to be pulled to allow you to blossom into your fullest, most authentic self? Also notice the dead plants from previous gardens. These too must be pulled or set aside. They may be dead, barely hanging onto life, or maybe they are still growing but do not fit into the vision you have for your new life garden. There is just not enough room to hold onto the plants that do not fit into the new garden theme. What are those things that need to be cleared out, or just set aside for now? Perhaps you can give them away to someone else to tend, or leave them dormant for now, to possibly bloom again later.

Make a list of your weeds and no longer viable plants so that you can clear your soil for the new garden.

When you are ready, slowly open your eyes and remembering your list of what needs to be cleared from your garden, and begin to paint, or draw your weed garden.

Process

Paint your garden of weeds that need to be pulled to clear the path for a new bountiful life. Draw the earth line. Draw in all the roots under the earth and all the weeds above the ground. Color and label your weeds and dead plants that you need to pull or set aside to make room for your next growth spurt so that you can blossom into your fullest most authentic self.

Weeding the Garden

Reflections

Reflections

Reflections

EXERCISE 8

PLANTING THE SEEDS

Materials

Seed packet template download from
https://barbarabustard.com/resources

Pencil, Colored Pencils, Markers

Tape or Glue

Meditation

Get comfortable. Take 3 deep cleansing breaths. Let all thoughts go. Relax your body. Check in to see if you are holding tension anywhere. Relax your shoulders if they are up around your ears, relax your jaw, release any tension you are holding in your body. Focus on your breathing and release any thoughts.

You are standing in your garden. You have pulled all the weeds and cleared all the dead away. The soil is rich and ready for planting. You can plant anything you want. What will it be? What plants do you need to grow and blossom for your life to be full and rich with life and color? What plants do you need to blossom into your full authentic self and achieve your vision? Look over your garden and picture your rows of seeds all marked by the seed packets. What are you growing and nurturing? Is it courage, or maybe patience?

Perhaps you need routine. What do you need to grow to feed your vision? What will this plant give you in order to live into your fullest, most authentic self? What instructions are on the packets to nurture and care for the plants so they will fully develop and bloom into the garden that will feed your dreams and desires for your life?

When you have walked all the rows and read all the packets slowly open your eyes and begin making your seed packets.

Process

Cut out and assemble your seed packets. Label the front top of your packets with the names of the plants you want to cultivate in your life. Write any notes or instructions on the back of the packet for caring for the seedlings so they will develop and grow. What image comes to mind that represents your plants? Draw the image on your packet or collage a printed image onto the packet.

Inside your packet put a note or words that may help you nurture your seedlings and remind you of what nutrients this plant gives you in order to grow and blossom.

Glue your packets on a popsicle stick and place them in potted plants around your house to remind you of what you are growing or plant them all in one flowerpot bouquet. When you need a boost to keep moving toward your life's vision, pick a packet and read your message.

"We can't become what we need to be by remaining what we are."

Oprah Winfrey

Planting the Seeds

Reflections

Reflections

EXERCISE 9

IN FULL BLOOM COLLAGE

Materials

9x12 Mixed Media paper
Cut out images from magazines or downloaded and printed
Pencil, Markers, Paint
Glue or Mod Podge
Whatever you would like to add to the collage

Meditation

Sit relaxed and close your eyes. Take three deep, cleansing breathes. In through your nose, down to your belly, and out through your mouth, exhaling completely. Release all tension from your body. Check in from your feet to your head and release any tightness. Focus on your breathing and release all thoughts.

It is a beautiful summer day and you are back in your garden. It is in full bloom! Look at all the beautiful growth that has happened. This is your most authentic life. What does it look like? What are all your dreams, wishes and goals for being the person you want to be? Look and see them all in full bloom. Wander through your Life Garden, soaking in all the beauty and wonder that is you. Snap pictures in your mind of you achieving all your goals. Stay and visualize yourself living your best, most authentic life as long as you want. When you are ready, slowly open your eyes, holding on to all the images, experiences, and feelings of joy and accomplishment that filled you as you walked through your Garden seeing yourself living your most authentic perfect life, and begin to create your collage.

Process

Paint or color the background. Draw, trace, paint, or collage images of you living your best, most authentic life! Have fun. There are no rules!

When you are finished, hang your collage where you can see it every day as a reminder of the amazing human being you are and have the potential to be.

BECOME THE PERSON YOU HAVE THE POTENTIAL TO BE!

In Full Bloom

The voice of your soul is breath.

Say it straight, simple and with a smile.

Live your dreams not your fears.

Compassion has no limit. Kindness has no enemy.

You must do the thing you cannot do.

Serenity

Grounded

SPIRITUALITY RENEWAL

COURAGE Strength

Connected to spirit

Prosperity

Family

Inner stillness is the key to outer strength.

Some people feel the rain, others just get wet. (Bob Marley)

You only lose what you cling to.

Health

Develop the power of listening.

May this day bring you PEACE, TRANQUILITY and HARMONY.

6/8/202

Reflections

Reflections

EXERCISE 10

- WRAP THE WORLD IN LOVE PRAYER FLAG

In 1971 The Hillside Singers wrote a jingle for Coca Cola which they then turned into a full-length pop song called "I'd Like to Teach the World to Sing" (In Perfect Harmony). The lyrics of the song create a vision of the world wrapped in love and peace.

The last verse is:
> I'd like to see the world for once
> All standing hand in hand
> And hear them echo through the hills
> For peace throughout the land

This song makes me think of Tibetan Prayer Flags, flying high in the mountains and letting the wind carry their prayers for love and peace throughout the World and Universe.

In 2005 we received an invitation in the mail. After being a couple for 25 years, our friends were finally able to be legally married in the State of Massachusetts. Included with the invitation were two rectangles of white fabric and a note requesting all invited to create a prayer flag with intentions for the couple and the world. Upon arrival at the wedding, the flags were strung high between poles which encircled the wedding party and all the guests so that the wishes, prayers and intentions could be carried by the wind to cover the Earth in love and good thoughts.

This is the practice and intention for Tibetan prayer flags.

You will make your own prayer flag or flags following a meditation.

Materials

Rectangle of white cotton fabric about 9"x12"
Paints, Permanent Markers
String for hanging

Meditation

Sit comfortably and take a few deep cleansing breaths to release all tightness and stress.

Let all thoughts go and focus on your breathing. Inhale through your nose slowly and deeply. Exhale slowly and completely through your mouth. Follow each breath with your mind's eye.

With your next breath inhale peace. Feel the sense of peace fill your lungs, heart, and whole body. Exhale any anxiety, fear, anger, or negativity. With every inhale, breathe in peace. With every exhale, envision the wind carrying that peace through the earth to every living being.

Now with your next breath, inhale love and let it fill your being with warmth, comfort, and joy. Feel the love wrapping around you like a soft blanket. With every exhale, send that love on the winds of change to envelope the Earth and all living beings with love.

When you are ready to return to the present, carry that love and peace with you and send it out to each person or being you encounter throughout the day. Send it through your thoughts to any person or place that you think of, friend or foe, particularly those who are the most difficult to love. Surround them with light and love.

Process

Paint the background of your fabric any way you like and using markers and paint, write your intentions, wishes and blessings for the World and the Universe on your flag. Add images as well if you like.

When your flag is completed, fold down the edge over a piece of string and glue it. Make sure you have enough string on both ends to tie the flag to a tree or your porch, or wherever it will hang and catch a breeze to carry your message. The flags are left to disintegrate and disperse their blessings being carried by the wind.

Prayer Flag

Reflections

Reflections

EXERCISE 11

Let's Get Zen and Doodle

There used to be a commercial on TV in the 70's for a bath powder called Calgon. The tag line for it was "Calgon, Take Me Away." It could just as easily be "Doodling, Take Me Away!" That's the healing power of your pen!

I carry a small notebook with me always. When I am sitting in the doctor's office, at the Department of Motor Vehicles, or anywhere that I have to wait, I pull out my little book and doodle! It passes the time and keeps me from stressing about the long wait or worrying about what the doctor will say. It is especially helpful while waiting for a dentist appointment! Going to the dentist as a child was very traumatizing and excruciatingly painful. Even though I now know that I will receive a medication that will numb my mouth and I won't feel the pain, I am still that frightened, anxious, child when I go to the dentist. Pulling out my little notebook and doodling takes me to a state of calm and relaxation while I wait. Doodling takes me away from stress for a while, when needed.

Doodling is drawing little shapes, designs, squiggles or patterns. No rules, just making marks on the paper. You most likely have doodled during meetings, or classes.

In the past, doodling has had a bit of bad rep. Think back to elementary school. Do you remember the teacher, or your parent, saying, "stop doodling and pay attention?" Well, guess what, you were paying attention while doodling! We now know that doodling is actually beneficial for our mental and physical health in several ways.

1. Doodling actually helps improve your retention of information. Research has shown that people who doodle while listening retain more information than those who just listened.

2. The repetitive motion of drawing calms your mind and gives it a rest from the stress of the world and everyday worries, thereby reducing your stress level. It only takes about 10 minutes a day to receive the benefits.

3. Doodling can help with problem solving. When you draw or doodle you are activating your creativity. Creativity is how we solve problems. Most problems have more than one solution and our creativity allows us to find different solutions.

4. Doodling will increase your creativity. Just like any creative activity, the more you do it, the more your brain will open new neural pathways and the more creative you will become.

5. Doodling like all art, helps us to know ourselves better. The repetitive action of doodling calms our mind and soothes us into a meditative-like state where our higher authentic self can reveal itself to us. Being in a meditative state provides insight into who we are, our authentic selves. We can receive insight into the person we have the potential to be.

As I said before, there are no rules for doodling. This is an art form everyone instinctively knows how to do! Just pick up your pen and draw whatever lines and shapes you want. In your next meeting or lecture doodle away while you are listening without guilt!

When you are not in class or a meeting, let Doodling take you away. Combining meditation with doodling puts you in a Zen state of mind and doodling becomes meditation.

The Merriam Webster dictionary defines Zen as:

> *a state of attentiveness in which one's actions are guided by intuition rather than by conscious effort ...*
> *Lost in the rhythm of the task at hand.*

When in this Zen state of mind, your mind is not occupied by thoughts or emotions and therefore open to everything.

Materials:

paper and pen

Meditation

Sit with your eyes closed, feet flat on the floor, hands still in your lap

Take a deep cleansing breath in through your nose, to the count of five, all the way down to the stomach. Hold for two and breathe out through your mouth slowly to the count of five. Repeat two more times, breathe in for the count of five, hold for two, out for the count of five.

Now in your mind's eye go to your favorite place to relax, It could be a quiet beach where you are alone or by a lake on a blanket in the soft grass. Go to wherever it is where you can get away, be at peace, and relax. Lay back and watch the clouds roll by in a beautiful blue sky. Let your thoughts roll by with the clouds. Just let them go and relax there in the quiet and peace. Connect with your Spirit and listen to any message you receive. Stay here in your special quiet place as long as you like, basking in the peace and tranquility.

When you are ready return to the present, slowly find your way back to the here and now, knowing that you can return to this place any time you need to. Slowly open your eyes.

Staying in your quiet, calm, meditative state, begin Zen doodling now.

Process:

On your paper make a border around the inside edge of your paper, it can be wavy or straight, no rules.

Next make a line from one side of the border to another side. The line can be straight, angled or curvy. Off of this line make another line to create a section. Continue dividing your area into sections with straight, curved, or angled lines.

You may also choose to draw the outline of a shape, animal, tree, body, etc., in the center of your paper and then proceed to divide this image into sections.

Next, just make a small doodle, any kind of doodle shape (circle, squiggle, leaf, spiral), in one corner of a section and repeat this doodle until it fills that section.

Move to another section and doodle until it is filled. Continue filling each section with a repetition of whatever doodle you choose for that section until you have filled all sections.

Next, fill in your border with solid black or a color of your choosing, if you like.

There really are no rules just let go and doodle your way to calm and peace.

"IMAGINE ALL THE PEOPLE LIVING LIFE IN PEACE,..."

JOHN LENNON

Zen Doodles

Reflection

Reflection

EXERCISE 12

SPLAT PAINTING

This exercise is pure fun! This is a meditation of Joy! You can return to that 5-year-old child who loved to make a mess and did not care how messy you got. Splat painting creates joy while doing it, and whenever you look at it.

You will want to do this outside. This activity is fun to do with a group of friends. Kids will want in on the fun as well. Splat painting is as much fun to watch as it is to do!

Materials

A hard surface – concrete, wood floor, the ground
Drop cloth unless you do not mind paint on your patio, driveway, lawn, or basement floor
Large sheet (at least 16"x20") of heavyweight watercolor or mixed media paper, or canvas board, or stretched canvas
Acrylic paints – lots of colors
Assortment of balls in various sizes and textures
Paint containers – Aluminum baking pans will work
Old clothes and shoes that you do not mind being spattered with paint, or bare feet

If you are using a stretched canvas, you will need to put books or blocks of wood, something hard inside the frame so that the canvas is supported and firm in order for the balls to bounce.

Meditation
ENJOY YOURSELF!

Process
If your paint is really thick, you may want to thin it slightly with a bit of water. Do not make it too thin though.

Grab a ball and dip it in one of the paint colors. Throw the ball down on the canvas and let it bounce and roll. Grab a different size and/or texture of ball and repeat with another color. Keep adding splats until you are happy with your painting. Have fun and let go.

If you really want your colors to pop, paint your canvas black first and let it dry before painting with the balls.

Hang your painting up. May it bring you joy.

Enjoy!

"Color! What a deep and mysterious language, the language of dreams."

Paul Gauguin

Splat Painting

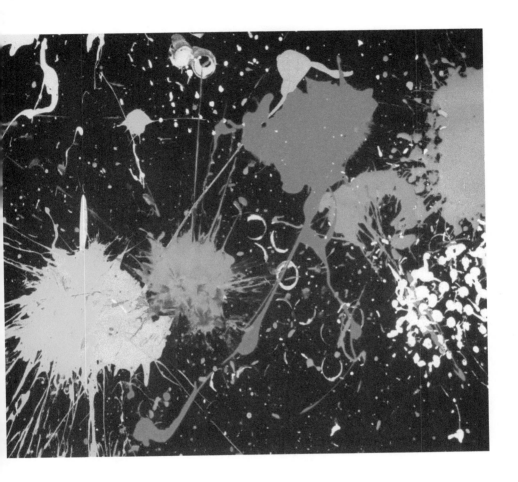

Reflection

Reflection

The

Exercise

Pages

"CREATE! THE HEALING
IS IN THE PROCESS"

Barbara Bustard

"THE DESIRE TO CREATE IS ONE OF THE DEEPEST YEARNINGS OF THE HUMAN SOUL."

DIETER F. UCHTDORF

Traditional Color Wheel

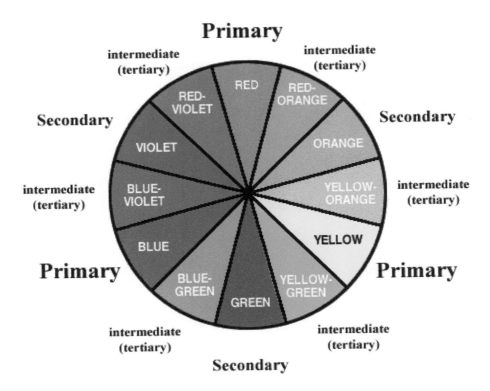

PLAY WITH COLOR

Color Wheel

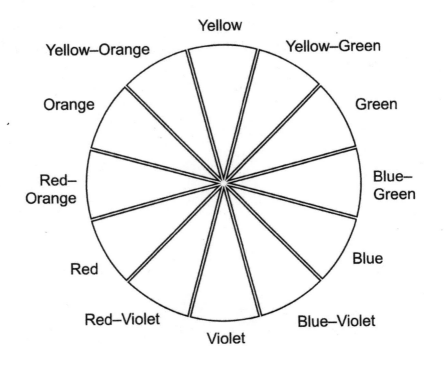

PLAY WITH COLOR

PLAY WITH COLOR

Exercise 1 – Your Emotional Color Wheel

Exercise 2 - Painted Prayer

Exercise 3 - The Winding Path

Exercise 5- Ruach- Breath of God

Exercise 6 – Finger Labyrinth

Exercise 7 – Weeding the Garden

Exercise 8 – Planting the Seeds

Front

Back

Front

Back

Exercise 9 – In Full Bloom

Exercise 10 – Wrap the World in Love – Prayer Flag

Exercise 11 – Zen Doodle

DRAW

JOURNAL

DOODLE

COLLAGE

PAINT

CREATE

CREATE

CREATE

CREATE

CREATE

CREATE

CREATE

CREATE

CREATE

CREATE

CREATE

CREATE

CREATE

CREATE

CREATE

CREATE

CREATE

CREATE

CREATE

CREATE

CREATE

CREATE

CREATE

CREATE

CREATE

CREATE

CREATE

CREATE

CREATE

CREATE

A HUGE THANK YOU TO ALL WHO MADE THIS BOOK POSSIBLE.

ACKNOWLEDGEMENTS

Judith, thank you for your constant and continued love, support, encouragement, and for being my cheerleader!

Thank you to my team: Michael R. Barton, Darden Ann Bennett, Joni Berman, Pam Bohlken, Tanya Chairavalle, Valentine Crouse, Laura Di Franco, Diana Fertsch, Annlyn Kisielewski Gomsak, Amy Heilman, Jeanne Kemp, Gail Kujawa, K C Lane, Kelly Langley, Denise Leblanc, Maria Guadelupe Lopez, Martha Montgomery, Alice Morris, Ginny Presley Robertson, Hope Salveson-Perkins, Robin Schmidt, Christy Smith, and Janette Stuart. I am so grateful for your gift of proofreading, feedback, and wonderful response to this book. Thank you for all of your help in launching this book into the world!

A HUGE thank you to my mentor and friend, **Laura Di Franco** for the generous gift of your time, knowledge, guidance, and inspiration to help me, and many others, put their brave words out into the world!

Thank you to all my students who inspire me every day!

TO MY DEAR READERS:

I hope that you found peace, serenity, joy, a spark of creativity and balm for your body, mind, and spirit in the creation of your meditative art. I thank you all for allowing me to share these healing art techniques with you.

NAMASTE

(The Divine in me acknowledges the Divine in you.)

About the Author

 Barbara Bustard is an artist, teaching artist, author, and the founder of Art for Body Mind and Soul. A graduate of Notre Dame University of Maryland, she holds a Bachelor of Arts Degree in Religious Studies and Art, as well as a Diploma in Color Therapy, and Certificates in Art Therapy for Self-Healing and Art Therapy for Self-Expression. Her mission is to promote the use of art for the benefits it provides in physical, mental, and spiritual well-being and the healing process. Barbara is also a contributing author in The Ultimate Guide to Self-Healing Series and an Inter-Faith Minister and Wedding Officiant.

When not teaching, making art, or writing, Barbara enjoys nature photography, always trying to capture the Extraordinary in the Ordinary. She and her wife Judith live in Baltimore, Maryland with their four cats, Stachie, Raisin, Noel and Lucky Bustard.

For information on meditative art sessions, you can contact Barbara through her website https://barbarabustard.com or Facebook https://www.facebook.com/artforbodymindandsoul/

For audio recordings of the meditations and other resources, please visit: https://barbarabustard.com/resources

To view her photography, please visit https://www.facebook.com/BarbaraBustardPhotography/